The Seven Deadlies

The Seven Deadlies

Poisons and Antidotes

Sermons by
Douglas Wilson

canonpress
Moscow, Idaho

Douglas Wilson, *The Seven Deadlies: Poisons and Antidotes*
Copyright ©2015 by Douglas Wilson

Published by Canon Press
P. O. Box 8729, Moscow, Idaho 83843
800-488-2034 | www.canonpress.com

Cover design by James Engerbretson.
Interior design by Valerie Anne Bost.

Unless otherwise indicated, all Scripture quotations are from the King James
Version.

Table of Contents

1 Sloth // 7

2 Covetousness // 17

3 Anger // 27

4 Lust // 37

5 Gluttony // 49

6 Envy // 61

7 Pride // 71

SLOTH

Go to the ant, thou sluggard; consider her ways, and be wise: Which having no guide, overseer, or ruler, provideth her meat in the summer, and gathereth her food in the harvest. How long wilt thou sleep, O sluggard? when wilt thou arise out of thy sleep? Yet a little sleep, a little slumber, a little folding of the hands to sleep: So shall thy poverty come as one that travelleth, and thy want as an armed man.
(Prov. 6:6–11)

INTRODUCTION

The seven deadly sins? Where does that categorization come from? The question can be addressed in two ways—historical and systematic. The historical question is the simpler of the two. Gregory the Great (late 6th century) is responsible for the list as we have it today. He saw the list in an order of increasing self-absorption. Sloth was the least offensive to God and Pride the most.

The list is not intended to compete with or supplant the Ten Commandments. It is simply a list, like other lists in the Bible. Each of these sins is mentioned in the Bible, but this list is not taking away from or supplanting the Ten Commandments. Proverbs 6:16 gives another list of seven sins that God really hates according to Solomon. But that list does not seek to compete with God's Ten Commandments either.

The list is simply an exercise in moral systematics—looking for a pattern in Scripture to help us understand a wide range of human disobedience. The Old Testament law does not tell us directly that the greatest commandment is to love the Lord your God with all your heart mind soul and strength, nor that the second is to love your neighbor as yourself. But Jesus tells us that that is what they are. The same is seen with the seven deadly sins: it is an exercise in systematics. You take the sins of the Bible, line them up and pick the ones that dominate the others, and order them in a systematic way. In this case we are taking the seven sins and organizing them in a particular order of evil or self-absorption. We do this while being careful not to supplant the Scripture or to put the "list" into competiton with the Word of God.

That said, the seven deadly sins are sloth, covetousness, anger, lust, gluttony, envy, and pride.

Review the passage at the beginning of this chapter (Prov. 6:6–11). In that place, sloth is contrasted with wisdom. The fool follows the path of sloth, while the man of God follows after wisdom. As industry has a fruitful harvest, so does sloth—poverty. When you sow brambles you cannot expect to harvest wheat. Whatever a man sows, that also he reaps. Sloth has alternatives to consider, compelling choices, like sleep and slumber. He says, "I need some sleep, I'm tired." Or, "You know it is awful hot today, maybe I'd better lay down here and wait for it to cool down a bit." Sloth is always filled with excuses and reasons why he can't get to the job, or even to the job site at all.

And lastly, the slothful are handled with considerable roughness. Poverty comes on the slothful man like an armed man. It comes to him like a mugger. This is how God designed the world to work. "The soul of the sluggard desireth, and hath nothing: but the soul of the diligent shall be made fat" (Prov. 13:4). This happens because the sluggard is hard to "get through to" and so God comes on him like an armed man.

PHYSICAL SLOTH

Physical sloth neglects the tools given to us for our physical provision. God provides for us by requiring us to provide for ourselves. But he does this in a world that is filled with abundance.

Preparation

A man has to work in order to be able to work. He has to work at plowing, for example, in order to be able to work the harvest. But the slothful have excuses at the first sign of work. "The sluggard will not plow by reason of the cold; therefore shall he beg in harvest, and have nothing" (Prov. 20:4). There are all sorts of reasons why such a man shouldn't plow: it is too hot, too cold, too wet. Whatever it takes to avoid the work, the sluggard comes up with reasons why he can't do the job. And in the end he cannot participate in the harvest, because he has not participated in the preparation for the harvest. This turns out to be perfectly fine with the sluggard, because he didn't want to do the work that was required for the harvest anyway. In the end however, poverty comes upon him like a thug and he must beg to eat.

Work

The biblical Christian understands that he was created for the work he finds in front of him (1 Thess. 4:11). And if he will not do it, then he should not eat (2 Thess. 3:10). This, unfortunately, he will hear more clearly than the words of a book like this. How does he know that he has been created for the work in front of him? That's where his hands are. God has created us so that we can work. And God has commanded us to use the tools he has given us and to work hard. Men and women achieve a true dignity in work and cannot be gained in any other way.

Testimony

"As vinegar to the teeth, and as smoke to the eyes, so is the sluggard to them that send him" (Prov. 10:26). When a sluggard is given a task to perform, it is astounding how many reasons come up for not carrying out the duty. But slothfulness is a public act. When the slothful are connected to others, as they frequently are, the word gets out. Their lack of work or refusal to work is news; the whole thing is public knowledge. People will talk about the lack of work—and they should. This is not gossip. Gossip is the passing on of unnecessary information to the detriment of others. Reporting on the slothful character of a sluggard is not gossip—it is actually helping the community. When a report says, "Bill is lazy and you shouldn't hire him," this is actually helping people to not be taken in by the sluggard. In the long run it even helps Bill. It is not gossip.

SPIRITUAL SLOTH

The reason for physical sloth is spiritual sloth. We don't understand what God has given to us in his word.

Physical sloth neglects the gifts God has given us to do whatever work He has given us to do his will. Spiritual sloth neglects the means of grace which God has so kindly provided us. The result of all such neglect is spiritual poverty. Just as physical sloth brings poverty with regard to finances and livelihood, so spiritual sloth brings on spiritual poverty—like a band of robbers.

Word of God

The Word of God is declared to you week after week. Do you prepare to hear it? Do you go to church prepared to hear the word of God? Do you know what psalms and hymns will be sung, and are you prepared to sing them? Just as you have to prepare in the physical realm you have to prepare to receive a harvest, so too in the spiritual realm do you have to prepare to receive a harvest. The Word of God is the source of the messages preached. What is your degree of familiarity with your Bible? God's people should be in love with God's book and they should know it inside out. They should be steeped in the truths contained in the Bible. And they should know it well enough that they are prepared to hear its exposition on Sunday mornings when they come together to worship God.

When we neglect the word of God, and as we neglect the Word of God, we find that God's word neglects us and poverty comes upon us.

Sacraments

Suppose you have not been baptized. Then believe and be baptized. Have you been baptized? Then improve on your baptism; live in terms of it. The mark of Jesus Christ is upon you. Has He invited you to His table? Do you come to sit down at His banquet without foresight or preparation? Do you make sure your children are prepared for worship and the meal? Do you dabble with the sacraments, or do you apply yourself to them? If you don't prepare or if you are not prepared, you are acting as a spiritual sluggard. Spiritual sloth has come upon you and spiritual poverty will come upon you.

Spiritual poverty

"The sluggard is wiser in his own conceit than seven men that can render a reason" (Prov. 26:16). The condition of the contemporary church is exactly this—the result of spiritual sloth. We are wise in our own conceits. Like the church in Laodicea (Rev. 3:14–22), we think we can see, but we are blind. We think we are rich, but we are poor with regard to the things of God.

We are impoverished and the worst thing is that we don't know we are impoverished. We don't have an understanding that this is our condition. Part of the reason is pressure from the unbelieving culture that is around us and our failure to withstand the pressure.

CALLING EVIL COOL

In times of cultural deterioration, pressure is always applied to invert the moral order. Isaiah 5:20 says, "Woe to those who call evil good and good evil." The world has always had lazy people, but historically they were always recognized as such. We live in a time when this sluggard-mentality is treated as something that should be praised. In 1950, the average fourteen-year-old kid had a vocabulary of 25,000 words. Today, the average kid has a vocabulary of 10,000 words, four of which appear to be *cable*, *X-Box*, *Netflix*, and *dude*. But how is this up and coming generation of the ignorati described to us in our public discourse?—street-smart, savvy, irreverent, and refreshing. Industry and diligence are mocked, and the baseball hat on backwards is the mark of a sage. We praise the lazy and exalt the sluggard. We do this even though we know that God mocks the ungodly, the lazy and those who refuse to work for what they desire. This means laziness is a sign of contempt for God.

THE ANTIDOTE TO THE SIN OF SLOTH

The danger of preaching against sin is that if it is heard wrongly, it turns us to ourselves. We hear a message on sloth, and are convicted of our sin. As a result, we resolve to work harder. But every glimpse of sin should always drive us to Christ. When we see our sinful hearts, our sinful behavior, it should drive us to Christ. It should not drive us to try to do better works or to be "less lazy." The law is a schoolmaster designed to turn us to Christ (Gal. 3:24–25). And when we recognize that our work (even our diligent work) is necessarily insufficient, the response should be to turn to the one who worked perfectly throughout His life.

Some men in John 6 came to Jesus and "said they unto him, What shall we do, that we might work the works of God? Jesus answered and said unto them, This is the work of God, that ye believe on him whom he hath sent (v. 28–29). Our work is to believe in the one whom God has sent (John 6:28–29). We can't do anything worthwhile unless the spirit of God is in us working his will out of us. He does this in us as we believe and trust in Him. This is the work of God, that we believe. All of our work should be a response of God working in us. It is the response of a life that trusts in the works of God in the earth. Jesus was born, lived, died, rose, ascended. When we believe this, this is the work of God. And it means that God is working in us. When this happens, we know that whatever we do, we do because God is working in and through us. Our theology comes out our finger tips.

The alternative to sloth and laziness is therefore Christ's work. When we believe in Christ, we work hard in the power of God.

COVETOUSNESS

What shall we say then? Is the law sin? God forbid. Nay, I had not known sin, but by the law: for I had not known lust, except the law had said, Thou shalt not covet. But sin, taking occasion by the commandment, wrought in me all manner of concupiscence. For without the law sin was dead. For I was alive without the law once: but when the commandment came, sin revived, and I died. (Rom. 7:7–9)

INTRODUCTION

The prohibition of covetousness shows us the authority of God's law over the inner man. The fact that this commandment nails us so completely perhaps accounts for our dislike of it.

In Romans 7 Paul is showing the point of the Law. In the first three chapters, he has shown that men are sinners, both Jews and Gentiles. Then, in chapter 4 and 5 Paul shows us that we are justified before God apart from works of the Law. Pharisaical Jews in the first century taught that the Law was central to salvation in an efficacious way. If you keep the law, you will earn God's favor. Paul is not diminishing the purpose or magnificence of the Law, but he is saying that the popular Judaic teaching of it in the first century was in error. The Law was/is important for salvation, but not in the way the first century Judaizer assumed. In chapter 7 he answers a different question: "If the Law was not given to save us, what was it given for?" His answer is that the Law was given to excite our sinfulness, to bring us to Christ, by revealing to us just how sinful we are.

The Law speaks to man in his sinful condition and shows us how corrupt and how in need of salvation from a source outside ourselves we are. The Law acts as a spotlight, revealing our sinfulness. The problem is not the Law (the spotlight). The light is not the problem, the dirt the light reveals is the problem. Paul isn't trying to get rid of the light; he is trying to shine the light all the brighter because he knows the light will shine on the sin and drive us to Christ. In verse 7 he asks, Is the Law sin? Is the Law the problem? He goes on immediately to say, no the problem is not the Law, the problem is the sin the Law reveals. If the Law hadn't come to reveal the sin, we wouldn't have known the sin existed. If the light hadn't come on, we wouldn't have known that the room was dirty.

Paul said if the Law had not come to show him his problem with lust, he would have gone on lusting and would have never known what was destroying his life. The purpose of the Law is to provoke sin, to reveal sin, to accentuate sin. Once the Law does its work, men are ready to hear about the Savior and to embrace him as their own.

We come now to the sixth sin—covetousness. This requires great attention because this is an area where we tend to sprinkle lavender water on our vices and call them virtues. We think that covetousness is something other than what God calls it. We think people are industrious, or hard working, or self controlled and driven (in a good way). We think at least they aren't slothful and lazy. We think we can't condemn a fellow for working hard just because he is covetous, but we can and we must. If a man is driven to do what he does because he is filled with covetousness, he is driven to sin by sin.

COVETOUSNESS

The sin of covetousness is discontent with what you have, a discontent which motivates you to yearn for what you do not have in a way contrary to the Word of God. It is contrary to the Word of God, and necessarily contrary, because it is the word of a competing god, an idol. Covetousness cannot be done in a godly way because it is the word of another god.

How can you go to the store and buy anything without coveting? You need to understand the desire to acquire in the light of the authority of the God you are serving. If you want "this item" so that you can glorify God more and more then you are not coveting at all. You are receiving God's gifts with thankfulness and are doing what you ought.

If, on the other hand, you cannot buy the object of your affections without trying to hide what you are donig from God, you are almost certainly involved in the sin of coveting. You are serving the god of your lusts—idolatry. If you can't afford the thing and you go home in order to mope, you have a problem with covetousness.

Here's a good way to check your heart: suppose you go to the store and see a thing you want to buy. Your thoughts suddenly go to wondering if you are being covetous and so you decide to go home and spend a few days thinking about the purchase. If something in you says, "No! I can't go home. What if someone comes and buys it before I can get back." You have the problem of covetousness. You need to go home and not come back at all. When you've got to have it, you aren't listening to God and you are coveting. Covetousness is a form of idolatry. And not surprisingly, God hates it (Is. 57:17).

The heart of the matter

The sin of covetousness is not caused by modern advertising. Our covetousness-inflaming advertisers do abound, but they have the good fortune to operate in a seller's market. The sinful heart wants to want things. "And he said, That which cometh out of the man, that defileth the man. For from within, out of the heart of men, proceed . . . covetousness . . . All these evil things come from within, and defile a man" (Mark 7:20–23). Covetousness is not imposed on you by mysterious forces outside you. Covetousness comes from within the heart of man. "They" have not created this sinful desire within your heart. They are appealing to it, but they have not created it. Jesus tells us that this sin requires a sharp lookout (Lk. 12:15). We have to understand that covetousness is problem that lives inside each of us.

Sexual covetousness

It is not an accident that one of the things listed in the tenth commandment is your neighbor's wife. You aren't to covet anything that you neighbor has, including his wife. This overlaps with another sin, which is of course lust, but covetousness still has to be understood separately. "Marriage is honourable in all, and the bed undefiled . . . Let your conversation be without covetousness; and be content with such things as ye have: for he hath said, I will never leave thee, nor forsake thee" (Heb. 13:4–5). It is not enough to say the marriage bed is honorable. The verse he goes on to say that in the marriage bed you must be content with what God has given you. You must be content with what you have because you have Him. You have Christ. What more could you possibly want?

The law of love

The man who covets does not love. The man who loves his neighbor refuses to covet If a man covets his neighbor's possessions, he does not love his neighbor. Covetousness is not a victimless activity. Covetousness shows and displays a lack of love for others. It is not something that is merely going on in your own heart or head. Owe no man any thing, but to love one another: for he that loveth another hath fulfilled the law. "For this, Thou shalt not commit adultery, Thou shalt not kill, Thou shalt not steal, Thou shalt not bear false witness, Thou shalt not covet; and if there be any other commandment, it is briefly comprehended in this saying, namely, Thou shalt love thy neighbour as thyself. Love worketh no ill to his neighbour: therefore love is the fulfilling of the law" (Rom. 13:8–10).

This whole list of sins shows that a person cannot do them and still love his neighbor. It also includes covetousness. If you love him, you will not covet things God has given him.

Cross fodder

Covetousness should be "cross fodder." Paul tells us to mortify our members which are upon the earth (Col. 3:5–7). One of our members which is on the earth is covetousness, a sin which keeps a lot of bad company (Jer. 22:17; Rom. 1:28–32). We need to get rid of all sin—including covetousness.

One of the central means which enables us to put this sin to death is the word of God. The Psalmist says, "Make me to go in the path of thy commandments; for therein do I delight. Incline my heart unto thy testimonies, and not to covetousness" (Ps. 119:35–36). There are two paths: you can incline yourself to covetousness or to God's path. You either trust what God says in his Word or you follow your own leanings and follow after not being satisfied with what God has given you. If you love to sing God's psalms and hear God's testimonies, you cannot hear another voice. If your heart inclines to the Word of God, you cannot hear another voice. Hearing God's testimonies rightly excludes covetousness.

By the same token, if your heart does not incline itself to God's word, it is inclining to covetousness. If you don't like to read the Word of God or if you cringe every time the opportunity to sing to the Lord comes along, you are coveting something. I don't know what you're coveting, but you are coveting somehow.

IN THE CHURCH

Just being involved in church or participating in Bible studies does not protect you from covetousness. Covetousness is not like regular participation in drunken orgies; it is commonly a respectable and very religious sin.

Hearers, not doers

According to James, when professing believers hear the Word of God but do not do it they deceive themselves (Jas. 1:22). But there is another kind of self-deception. In Ezekiel 33 the prophet tells us, "And they come unto thee as the people cometh, and they sit before thee as my people, and they hear thy words, but they will not do them: for with their mouth they shew much love, but their heart goeth after their covetousness (v. 31). One of the reasons for their self-deception is that their heart goes after covetousness. The tendency is to hear the word of God, but not do it. Don't judge yourself according to your willingness to listen to the Word of God only. Realize that people can love to listen to the Word of God, but it is when you hear it but don't do it that covetousness takes control. You profess to love with your mouth, but your heart is going after covetousness.

Least to greatest

Covetousness shows itself in as many ways as there are people. Rich, poor, male, female, Asian, Caucasian; It doesn't matter who you are. Covetousness comes to everyone alike; from the least to the greatest. When covetousness grips a people, the leaders of the church are not immune (Jer. 6:13; 8:10). Even the leaders of the nations are not immune from covetousness. The leaders reflect the kind of people who are under them. If the people are covetous, the leaders are covetous. We get the kind of leaders we deserve.

Making merchandise

The lake of religious faith is a place where the covetous learned to fish a long time ago. When people have religious faith, covetous men flock to the simple and gullible people of faith. Second Peter tells us, "And through covetousness shall they with feigned words make merchandise of you: whose judgment now of a long time lingereth not, and their damnation slumbereth not" (2 Pet. 2:3). The shepherds of the flock are to feed the sheep, not fleece them. This is so common that true teachers of the Word must take special care to live in a way that is completely above reproach (1 Thess. 2:5). Even when the offering is given in accordance with the Word, assurances are still necessary (2 Cor. 9:5).

THE POLITICS OF COVETOUSNESS

It is remarkable how the Bible addresses this sin of covetousness the realm of what we would call politics.

Qualified for office

When we come to choose men for political office, one of the things the Bible requires is that we find men who hate covetousness (Ex. 18:21). It is not enough simply to have avoided personal covetousness. Before he is put into a position of power and compulsion, he must be a man who hates covetousness. He will destroy the culture if he does not. He will pillage the nation and raise taxes until the country is destroyed. When civil rulers do not hate covetousness, the alternative is great oppression.

The alternative

"The prince that wanteth understanding is also a great oppressor: but he that hateth covetousness shall prolong his days" (Prov. 28:16). The contrast is made between the prince who lacks understanding and is a great oppressor and the one who hates covetousness. Covetousness in public office produces the theft of the resources of the people. The man who hates stealing, hates covetousness and will hate stealing from his people. We need to elect officials who hate the idea of pillaging other people's money.

THE ANTIDOTE TO ALL SIN

Just as the solution to our sloth is not our works the answer is Christ's works. In a similar way, the solution to our covetousness is not our acquisitions or our resolve to not acquire anything. Rather, it is to realize what we have in Jesus Christ. One of the more interesting passages in Paul's letters is this one: "Therefore let no man glory in men. For all things are yours; whether Paul, or Apollos, or Cephas, or the world, or life, or death, or things present, or things to come; all are yours; and ye are Christ's; and Christ is God's" (1 Cor. 3:21–23). How can we be covetous? What is there to gain? Everything is ours in Christ. If we are acquiring things in Christ, we are acquiring things that already belong to Christ and therefore to us. If we understand this, the game is entirely different. We are stewards of what God gives us, not autonomous owners. We are to do whatever we do to the glory of God. We don't need to *ache* to get things. Everything belongs to him and everything we need belongs to us because we belong to Christ. If we are hungry and the food is not present, since it all belongs to God, we can be content to realize that we are getting what we need in Christ. We can give thanks to him for whatever circumstance he has us in. Christ owns everything and gives us every good thing.

ANGER

And grieve not the holy Spirit of God, whereby ye are sealed unto the day of redemption. Let all bitterness, and wrath, and anger, and clamour, and evil speaking, be put away from you, with all malice. And be ye kind one to another, tenderhearted, forgiving one another, even as God for Christ's sake hath forgiven you. (Eph. 4:30–32)

INTRODUCTION

As we have known for centuries, anger is a brief madness. When it is not a godly anger, anger is not rational. And when a man comes to his senses again, after a fit of anger, he has plenty of leisure to repent of the damage he has done. But repairing the damage is often far more difficult than the mere desire to repair it. It is easy to lament the damage that was done, but repairing it is a different thing entirely. That is not to say that the damage cannot be repaired. Christ was sent into the world to repair all sin, and craters left by anger are not outside God's grace.

In our text we see a list of sins that grieve the Holy Spirit of God. When Christians talk in ways that demean and tear down other Christians, the Holy Spirit of God is grieved. Consequently, as followers of Christ, we desire to reject all these sins—wrath, anger, malice, clamor. But we can't just reject certain ungodly behaviors. If we cast out a demon without replacing it with something better, we don't solve anything. It is not enough to reject the sin alone. We must also embrace kindness, tenderheartedness, and forgiveness. We must replace the sin with godly virtues. We must put on the Lord Jesus Christ.

RIGHTEOUS ANGER

Sins differ from one another. Sometimes the sin is an unrighteous counterpart to a righteous behavior. For example, adultery is a perversion of the righteous action of loving your wife. Other times the sin is something that should be done, but in a different way. Adultery is never a good thing. But in the case of anger, there is righteous anger and there is unrighteous anger. And it is not biblical to make a blanket statement and say, "don't be angry," because there are times when being angry is the godly thing to do.

In our generation there is a great antipathy toward righteous anger, but we see various examples of righteous anger throughout Scripture. We see God being angry, various saints being angry; we see Christ being angry in the Scripture. But our generation has disliked, hated, and rejected the scriptural teaching on anger and consequently has rejected the notion of righteous anger. One of the reasons why we have so much unrighteous anger in our lives is because we do not believe the authority of the Bible about the real thing. Unless we have some biblical idea of what godly anger looks like, we will have no way to repent of our ungodly angers.

Jesus was angry

First, we are called to be like Jesus Christ in every area of His life and in our lives. We are to love like Jesus Christ, to respond to the various situations we run into like Jesus Christ—we are to be like our teacher. When Jesus was presented with the man with a withered hand as a trap, His response was one of anger and grief (Mk. 3:5). The text never tells us that He was angry when He cleansed the Temple, although He probably was. His actions showed that he likely was angry, but the text doesn't tell us specifically that he was angry. But in the incident of the man with a withered hand, we are told explicitly that Jesus was angry.

So in this passage, consider three things about His righteous anger—the occasion for it, what accompanied it, and the results of it.

First, the Lord Jesus was angry because the people were so bound up in their own rules and regulations that they were going to set Christ up to see if he would break their laws. They wanted to see if Jesus would break their Sabbath laws in order to heal the man with the withered hand. It was their pomposity, their self-righteousness, their self concern that caused them to create laws that went far beyond the laws God gave us. They were so full of themselves that they didn't care that the man needed help, no matter what day it was. Jesus Christ was angry because the religious leaders, those who should have known better, cared more about their own rules than they did about God and His desires. We are angered by a student tapping a pencil on a desk or looking at us funny. What made Jesus Christ angry was hostility to kindness. We are angry because we don't want to be kind;

he was angry because others refused to be kind to one another. So, the occasion for anger was very different from what normally happens with us.

Second, the thing that accompanied anger in Jesus' case was grief. He was angry and grieved. He was not angry and eager to wound. He was not angry and eager to hurt. It was grief that accompanied his anger.

Finally, the results of Jesus' anger was that a man was healed. When we get angry, we destroy things. When Jesus was angry, he restored things to be the way they ought to be. He healed; we wound. We need to imitate the Lord Jesus in everything and this includes the way He responded to things that caused him to be angry.

The anger of God

We must remember that a great deal of what we see around us every day makes God angry and keeps God angry. "He that believeth on the Son hath everlasting life: and he that believeth not the Son shall not see life; but the wrath of God abideth on him" (John 3:36). We need to have this important doctrinal category. When a man remains in unbelief, the wrath of God abides on him. The wrath of God has not yet fallen upon him fully, but the wrath of God is resting on him. It is hanging over him and it will come upon him at some point (certainly by the last day).

It is important for us to remember this teaching lest we fall into the easy idea that God is a grandfatherly figure in the sky who squints at the world from a distance and has a sugar coated view of life here on earth. Of course when horrible things like the Holocaust come along, He is not pleased. But when it comes to us and our behavior, he is pretty happy with us overall. He does not superintend the world, or judge us or the thoughts and intentions of our hearts. But the Bible says He does judge the thoughts and intentions of men's hearts. He does see the unbelief that is exhibited on every hand. And that unbelief angers God.

Men also need to know that the only way to avoid the anger of God is in the Cross of Jesus Christ. The problem with the leaders in Christ's day is the same as the problem with our generation. We say, "I could never serve a God like that," so we make up our own gods and worship them. It never occurs to us that we need to worship the God who is, the God who lives rather than the god we've created in their own image. What we are saying is, "I make my own idols. Thank you very much." We cannot hold to this and to the Scriptures at the same time. The Bible is full of examples where God's anger and wrath are poured out upon sinners who reject the knowledge of God. And there is only one refuge from the wrath of God and that is in the wrath of God poured out on Jesus Christ on the cross of Christ.

We are commanded

Be angry, the Bible commands us, but do not sin (Eph. 4:26). We are commanded to be angry. This is just a few verses before our text where we are told to put away all wrath and anger. The Bible tells that there are circumstances when we should be angry and it commands us to be angry in those circumstances, but we are not to sin in those circumstances when we are angry.

Ephesians 4:26 tells us that when we are angry we not to sin and when we are angry we are not to let the sun go down on our anger. So even if the anger is righteous, like manna, it will not keep overnight. If your anger is righteous, you must put it away before sundown. If you don't it will turn to something else before morning.

In Ephesians 4:30–32 you are to put your sin away right away. You are not to tolerate sin for a moment. But anger that is righteous, you are to act on and put it away before the sun sets that day. This is because we are sinners and righteous anger can and will become corrupt overnight. There are many things in our culture that should make us angry (abortion, sodomy, lying politicians, adulterers, fornicators, etc.). But if you hang on to your anger too long it will turn into bitterness or some other vile sin. You need to get rid of your righteous anger before the sun sets.

One or the other

Another thing to consider in this discussion is the flow of argument between Romans 12:19 and chapter 13:6. Do not avenge yourselves (v. 19), but leave room for wrath. He is not telling us to avoid vengeance because vengeance is wrong, but because vengeance belongs to God. It is God's responsibility to avenge the wronged, not ours. We need to maintain the idea of vengeance and justice. God is a just God and vengeance belongs to Him. So we need to understand that vengeance is God's, not that vengeance is wrong.

How does He do this? And who is the agent of such wrath? The magistrate is God's deacon in this

(13:4). God has set up powers in the earth to take care of his people and to carry out vengeance. So, we are to treat our enemies with love and care (Rom 12:20–21), while God's agents carry out God's wrath on our behalf.

Even though our civil authorities are not doing what God has appointed them to do, this does not change what God has commanded us to do. While we wait for godly authorities we should do what God has commanded us to do, and at the same time we should tell the civil authorities to do what God has commanded them to do. "God has appointed you to carry out his wrath on evil doers and to reward those who live godly and righteous lives."

Unrighteous Anger:

Our most common problem, however, is not one of how to deal with all our righteous anger.

Works of the flesh

We need to realize that unrighteous anger is a work of the flesh. Like the other sins we are considering, this one keeps bad company as well. It is one of the works of the flesh (Gal. 5:20). People whose lives are characterized by this do not inherit the kingdom (v. 21). You cannot tolerate that kind of sin in your life and expect to be received by God on the last day. Everyone who receives God's forgiving grace also receives God's sanctifying grace. If you've received his forgiving grace, your life will change. If your life hasn't changed you haven't received forgiving grace. You are still in your sins.

Put it off

In our text from Ephesians, we are told to put our wrath and anger away. We are also told to put it off in Colossians 3:8. The Ephesians and Colossians were taught from the very beginning to put away these attitudes. Unrighteous anger and wrath are not in keeping with a godly Christian life. You were taught in the beginning to cut it off, and you are being taught now to put it off. You are not your own; you were bought by someone else. If you were ransomed by Jesus Christ, you were bought by Him and consequently don't belong to yourself—you belong to Him. He has told you to get the anger out of your life, and he has been telling you this from the beginning. You have been told to put on Christ. You must be like Christ if you have put him on.

Excuses

Note what the text says to all followers of Christ—put it away. It does not say put it away *if* . . . Some people think you can't teach an old dog new tricks. "I'm too old to change." "I've been like this my whole life." You may think you are not young enough to change, the provocations are too big for you to change, and so forth. But the word must be bluntly spoken to every follower of Christ—knock it off. You have been born again, into a new life—Christ's life. You must be like him.

Getting underfoot

People who are angry often claim to have been provoked to anger. They say, "I never would have gotten so angry, if…" Or they might say, "My anger solved the problem. It fixed the sin that provoked me in the first place." But the Bible says, "the wrath of man worketh not the righteousness of God" (Jas. 1:20). Your unrighteous anger doesn't fix anything. Your anger does not fit the biblical command to have someone spiritual restore the brother who is caught in a sin (Gal. 6:1). This is because the text also says that the spiritual brother must do the restoring gently. If you are angry, you are not qualified to restore anyone in a gentle way. You are not qualified to restore anyone at all, because you are in need or restoration yourself.

If your children are disobedient, you need to discipline them when they first disobey, long before you are tempted to be angry. If you are angry, you are not qualified to discipline them. You must discipline them when you do not feel like it. This is the only time in the process when you are qualified to discipline them. So, discipline your children after the first act of disobedience and not after the fifth time when they finally raise your ire to the point where you feel like you want to discipline them.

Second, you need to remember that your behavior is a model to your children and family of how they are to live their lives. Jesus Christ just told you not to be angry. So you need to demonstrate to your children how commands are to be obeyed, not how commands are to be safely disregarded in the home. When you disobey God, your children say to themselves, "If Dad doesn't obey God, why should I obey Dad?" You need to remember that your children are learning how to be obedient, or not, from how you are obedient to God, or not.

Third, remember the passage from James above, "the wrath of man worketh not the righteousness of God" (Jas. 1:20). Not only are you not qualified to correct a brother, because you are in need of correction yourself, but this also means that your anger interferes with a biblical solution with whatever it is that angers you. Let's assume your family is a mess. Your wife is not respectful to you, your children are disobedient, there really is sin in your home. But your anger does not solve the problem, it actually gets in the way of God's work. Your anger interferes with God's righteous solution to your problems. Your anger actually complicates the mess, and it might well turn out to have been the source of the whole mess.

Seed form

In our life together, we must note that anger frequently grows up from what we think are lesser sins—annoyances, irritations, resentments, gripes, imputations of motive, and so forth. So you might think you don't have a problem with this because you never throw anything, you don't yell and hit anyone or anything. But there are men who can communicate their displeasure and anger simply by their manner or by their demeanor. They might walk off or become very quiet. They don't verbalize their anger, but they do make it plain. And this sort of anger is just as damaging to the home as the kind where things fly around the room. There is such a thing as sullen anger.

When the father acts in this way, he never talks out his anger, or confesses his sin of anger, the children grow up never expressing their resentment, or their disgust with their father's religion. They simply drift off when they grow up, and no one knows what the problem really is.

Tenderhearted

What is the counterpart to every form of ungodly anger? It is kindness, tenderheartedness, forgiveness to one another. This is the only measuring rod you may use. You may not say, "I wasn't angry because I didn't throw anything." You must instead say, "I was kind." "I was considerate." "I was tenderhearted." The absence of outward anger is not the same thing as the presence of Christ's character. If you are living like Christ, you must exhibit his characteristics and these include forgiveness and kindness, not anger, nagging, backbiting, and bitterness. There are two ways to go: you can either be hardhearted or you can be tenderhearted.

THE ANTIDOTE TO ALL SIN

If we are going to "fix" these problems or any of the sin problems in this series we've got to resolve in our minds to correct them, not by our own works, decisions, and resolutions, but by putting on Christ and the Gospel. We can't look to ourselves to solve the problem. We need to know that obedience to the Law, thou shalt not be angry, cannot be done in our own strength and in our own might. We got ourselves into this pit and the only thing we can do in that process is to dig deeper. We must instead look to Jesus Christ.

In order to be freed from our own fits of anger and rage, we must contemplate through faith the greatest display of wrath in the history of the world—the cross of Jesus Christ. The solution to wrath is wrath. You must look to the greatest act of wrath in history and meditate on it—the cross of Christ. There, in the wrath of God, the petty wrath of all His people was crucified. In the cross of Jesus Christ, your anger died. It died because God in his anger killed it. The solution to our anger is not our lack of anger. The solution to our fits of anger is God's wrath with that anger. We must look at the cross for God's solution to wrath.

"Much more then . . . we shall be saved from wrath through him. For if, when we were enemies, we were reconciled to God by the death of his Son" (Rom. 5:9–10).

So we were saved from wrath by wrath. And if we have no glimpse of true wrath, we will spend our lives face down in the puddles of our own private animosities. Dear God, deliver us! But deliverance is only through the cross. You will be delivered from anger only by seeing how angry God was with it. And that is seen through the cross.

LUST

Mortify therefore your members which are upon the
earth; fornication, uncleanness, inordinate affection,
evil concupiscence, and covetousness, which is idolatry. (Col. 3:5)

INTRODUCTION

It is important to point out two things before we begin. First, notice the reference to the members which are
upon the earth. What is meant by this phrase? It means
because we are related to Adam, we have remaining sin.
Even though we are converted people, with a new nature within us (we are new creations), while we remain
in the flesh we still have a collision with the spirit (Gal
5:17). We need to understand that this particular sin
is not one that comes at us from the outside. We have
within us members which have a natural propensity to
sin. Therefore, even though we are Christians, we need
to put to death these members which are still upon the
earth.

Second, in verse 7 it tells us that we used to walk
according to these things. It is important to realize that
the world is full of these kinds of evil behaviors. Our

children are being taught about immorality and fornication at every turn and in every context. We cannot
get our children through a day without attempts by the
world to teach them about life and how it is to be lived.
We need to know this and how to come against this as
Christians who live intelligently in the world.

So, how do we go about mortifying our members
that are upon the earth? How are we to think as Christians when we come into these temptations? We do not
live in a time of public silence on lust. There has been no
moratorium on the noise about it, the perpetual chat-
ter that surrounds us on every side. Enticements to lust,
discussions of lust, inducements to lust, are all constant.

TRICKS OF THE TRADE

Contrary to biblical evidence, and contrary to the
society around us, we have assumed that lust is a male
problem. We think that only men have a problem when
it comes to lust. Well, of course life is different for men
and for women—men love to want, while women desire
to be wanted. It is not as though men have a problem
with lust and women do not. The two sexes actually have
complementary problems with this sin. When men look
at a scantily-clad woman walking by, or when they look
longingly at the covers on the magazine rack, it is because they have this problem. A man can't help the first
look, but he can help looking again. And he can help
thinking about what he saw later in the day or the next
week. When he does that, when he lingers over it, we
say, he has a problem with lust. Correspondingly when
women behave and dress to be looked at, they have the
complementary problem also. This is why the Bible tells

women to be modest in the way they dress (1 Tim. 2:9).

Dresses like a hooker

First let us consider what we learn about this from Proverbs 7:1–23. What are the characteristics of feminine lust? First, the woman described dresses like a hooker (v. 10). We need to take care here, because much of this modern hooker-wear has already been mainstreamed, and is for sale at a fine store near you (v. 10). Christian moms buy such things for their daughters. The stores and the culture tell us that dressing like a prostitute is normal and is the style. Dressing immodestly is the norm in our culture.

Does this mean that a Christian woman must dress in a dowdy fashion like Minnie Pearl with long sleeves and high neck? Not necessarily. But if the choice is between dressing like a hooker and dressing like a prude, erring on the side of modesty is to be preferred. But this is not the only choice. A Christian woman can (and must work hard to) dress fashionably (to a point) and also dress modestly. And Christian women must resolve in their minds to fight the surrounding culture and be careful not to dress to be noticed in a particular way. If for some reason you cannot dress both modestly and in fashion, you must make up your mind that you will dress unfashionably. It is a characteristic of the woman with a problem with lust that she dresses in a provocative way.

Subtle, tangled heart

Second, the woman with a problem with lust is subtle and has a tangled heart (the end of verse 10). She is crafty, and knows how to set and bait the trap. Because of this subtle approach, she also has what is called deniability. In other words, she has the room to draw herself up and act insulted when someone points out that what she is wearing is less than modest: "What do you think you're saying? I'm not that kind of girl." But if you aren't that kind of girl, don't advertise like you are that kind of girl. The subtle act of deniability means that she can say, "I didn't mean it that way. That isn't what I meant." But ultimately what was intended isn't really important—what is put on and worn outside speaks loudly enough and the response just reveals a tangled heart. A woman is responsible for what she says about herself when she dresses. The Bible says that at some level of the heart, no matter what is said about it verbally, is what was meant. The woman with the problem of lust dresses in a provocative way, sets various stratagems to attract attention, and also does it in a way that she can deny that it was done on purpose. But according the Word of God, the denial is not true.

Stubborn, headstrong

Third, when it is pointed out what she is doing, she does not have the frame of heart to hear it. It doesn't matter who points it out to her: the pastor from the pulpit, her mother, her friends. She is brash, loud, and stubborn (v. 11). How can you tell when a woman fits into this category? Well, what is her response if mom says her jeans are too tight? Is she quiet and gentle about that opinion, or does she get louder and throw the comment back into her mother's face? If she is argumentative about it, that reveals the sin. If she says, "that's just your interpretation," to use an old-fashioned word, she just needs to repent. If she responds with "thank you

very much for telling me," she is probably
doing okay. If there is argument between a parent and
daughter over what she is wearing, that displays a problem with lust just as much as if her brother is lusting
after immoral pictures on the web. In the same way we
would say that a young man ogling all the girls needs
to have a talk with his father, so too does a woman who
dresses like she wants the ogling.

Wanders away from home
Fourth, she goes wandering in the evening. God put
the sun up for a reason. The daytime is when we are sup-
posed to work and take care of business. Evening is not
for playing with your friends; it's for sleeping. You get
into trouble when you resist God's ordained pattern for
living. He put the sun in the sky to govern things that
ought to be done and he put the moon in the sky to tell
us when it is time to rest from the well-lit part of the day.
Sexual sin gravitates to dark places at dark times of the
night. The woman with a lust problem doesn't like it at
home. Home is boring (v. 11).

Sexually aggressive
Fifth, she is the text says she approaches the young
meathead and makes the proposition verbal. The proposition has been made all along, by the way she dresses
and acts (but she could still deny it). Now, she is sexually
aggressive (v. 13). She doesn't have deniability now, but
now the hook is in.

Lots of promises
She promises him a good time, as countless popular songs put it, "all night long" (v. 18). She makes lots

of promises, along with flattery. She says, "Your life will be so much better if you come away with me. You will be so happy to come with me, and do it with me."

Flattery

Finally, her words drips with honey; she knows how to use pseudo-respect (v. 21). We need to learn about sex and sexual relations from the Word of God, not the radio and the television. She is offering two things men aren't getting at home—sexual excitement and respect. There are too many Christian wives who don't understand the first thing about sexual things, but the harlot does. The harlot can give him everything he wants or thinks he wants. Many wives don't respect their husbands, but the prostitute can give him pseudo-respect. She tells him he is so smart and strong and wonderful. You know she's setting a trap because she's saying it to the guy in verse 7—the guy we called a fathead earlier. She is religious. She's paid her vows.

This is not a problem that only men have, it is a problem that every son of Adam has and every daughter of Eve has. So in order to avoid the problem, we need to learn self-control so you don't even begin to go down that road.

MEN WITH NO SENSE

Lust is not a sensation; it is a road with an established destination. You cannot keep going down the road that you are on without getting to the destination at the end of the road. There is no getting off the road without self-control and repentance. That destination is always some form of sexual immorality.

Flee, abstain

Paul tells Timothy to flee youthful lusts (2 Tim. 2:22). We often want to agonize all night in prayer about it and have God give us some spiritual magic. But Paul tells Timothy to run away—flee youthful lusts. Peter tells us to abstain from fleshly lusts which war against the soul (1 Pet. 2:11). These whisperings, intimations, and suggestions are not your friend. They will wreck your life. They will wreck your marriage. They will wreck your relationship with your children. Peter tells us these things war against your soul. They want to kill you. They want to destroy you. Abstain from them. Do not fraternize with the enemy.

Whenever Potiphar's wife starts to unbutton her blouse, in whatever form she shows herself, both Peter and Paul say run away. Don't try to try to figure out how close you can get to the sin without actually falling into it. Once you start enjoying the thrill of the temptation, you have already fallen for it. This means you should avoid girls who dress immodestly, drastically alter the movies you watch, have nothing to do with porn on the net, and so forth. No one ever asks how many slugs they can have on their salad before it ruins the salad. Just so, no amount of immorality is good for a man's life. You cannot get right up to the edge without sinning. If you flirt with that kind of danger you have already fallen to the temptation. This means the only thing left for you to do is to run away.

Consider the end

The young man in Proverbs did not think or consider the results (7:7, 22–23). He was not thinking through the long term consequences. He went after her like an ox to the slaughter. This sort of lifestyle will lead to death, to destruction. The way that seems right to a man actually leads to death. Stay away from the cliff edge. Run away. Do what the Bible says to do. Put up barriers, boundaries and walls.

Whose disciple?

The world teaches on this subject all the time. How many of these lessons have you mastered, and how much of the Bible's teaching on lust, sex, marriage, etc. have you studied? How can you prepare for marriage, or teach your wife, when you refuse to learn? The single man needs to prepare himself to be married. He does not have the same help that the married man does, but the single man can practice the same kinds of help that the married man has.

THE GREATEST EARTHLY HELP

The grace of God is not necessarily heavenly. The solutions that God provides are not necessarily the kind that we might normally expect in terms of heavenly versus earthly. We must set our minds on Christ, seated at the right hand of the Father, but in doing this, we heed His word. There are three things to be said here. All three apply to married people and two of them apply to single people.

The marriage bed is to be honored

First, the author of Hebrews tells us plainly that the marriage bed is to be honored (Heb. 13:4). We are to think highly of the marriage bed. We are to esteem it, set it on a pedestal. We are not to profane the marriage bed.

This means that sexual living is to be highly esteemed among Christians. When we refer to sexual activity and marital love we are not embarrassed or appalled by it. The thing that should distress us is immorality, not sex. We don't object to art when we object to art vandalism. In the same way, when we object to sexual vandalism we are not objecting to marital sex.

Single Christians can carry many sexual sins into marriage unless they manage their sexual behavior now. You honor your future husband or wife now by protecting yourself as a single person now.

The marriage bed is to be used

Second, the world is filled with immorality, and the apostle Paul tells that one of the functions of marriage in a fallen world is to help guard against temptations to immorality (1 Cor. 7:2–3). The marriage bed is to be used. The world is filled with immorality and one of the functions of the marriage bed is to help men and women avoid the problems of sexual temptation.

Of course sex was created before sin entered the world, but once it did enter the world, marriage was used by God to protect the marriage bed.

The marriage bed is to be a delight

Finally, the godly man is commanded to be satisfied with his wife's breasts, and is to be ravished with her love (Prov. 5:19). The marriage bed is to be a delight. Christian men should give themselves to their wives and wives to their husbands with great joy. It is to be looked forward to and anticipated. It should be held in high esteem and thought of in the same way an adventure is looked forward to.

This is a help to single people because they can't look forward to something they have been engaged in trashing for years and years. Your ability to give to your future wife or your husband shows itself in how you treat the marriage bed now. You should think of marriage very highly now and dwell on how wonderful it will be without doing things that will ruin the great joy in the future.

THE ANTIDOTE TO ALL SIN

If you are in the grip of this temptation, if you fall all the time to this temptation, if you are discouraged by how easily this temptation overtakes you, you need to know that you cannot overcome the temptation to lust by making resolutions. You cannot deliver yourself from this sin. But as Christians, we must go beyond earthly means, even those earthly means given to us by God. Under Christ, such things are helps, but not ultimate solutions. As we have seen with the other sins we have considered, the solution is not new resolutions, but rather Christ. If we don't consider Christ rightly, being physically married doesn't help us. Running away from the temptation doesn't help us at all. They only help if they are subordinated to your healthy worship of the true and living God. The final antidote to lust (no matter what your situation or station in life) is not to extinguish desire from our hearts, but rather to direct it rightly—to the living God, the font of all pleasure. We are not to squelch our desires. The problem is that our desires are too tiny. We need to desire more, to desire union with God. We must learn to love God, at whose right hand is pleasure forevermore (Ps. 16:11). We need to dwell on and pursue the fact that we are united to Christ. When God sees us committing sexual vandalism and He condemns it, he is not saying no because he has discovered someone having a good time and he wants to stop him. That is not the biblical view of God and it is not how He thinks about His people or pleasure. At God's right hand are pleasures forevermore. What you are doing by these destructive behaviors is making yourself stupid so that you cannot see that God pours out blessings, joy, pleasure, everlastingly on his children. Our desire is not inflamed—frankly it is anemic. The Christian is someone who wants to be with the living God world without end.

GLUTTONY

Know ye not that the unrighteous shall not inherit the kingdom of God? Be not deceived: neither fornicators, nor idolaters, nor adulterers, nor effeminate . . . Meats for the belly, and the belly for meats: but God shall destroy both it and them (1 Cor. 6:9–20).

INTRODUCTION

We must begin with an important qualifier. This chapter is not about that second helping of mashed potatoes at Thanksgiving. At the same time, the issues surrounding gluttony remain important ones. Gluttony does not refer to a simple desire to eat and drink, but rather to an inordinate desire. And when we use words like inordinate, we have to remember to ask the fundamental question—by what standard? It is important to remember that in the Bible there are only two tables: You either eat at the table of the Lord Jesus Christ or you eat at the table set by demons. If you understand that fact rightly, everything you do will be incorporated into that understanding. We need to understand food in a distinctively Christian manner. What does the Bible teach about food and our relationship to it?

Gluttony does not refer to a desire for food and drink. We are not Gnostics. God made food, matter, everything. He created us to eat and to desire to eat. When He created it, He pronounced it good. We are not permitted to call what God calls good, evil. Not everything that is fallen is evil. Although our bodies are good, they are fallen and though God created food good, it is fallen. And we have to take this into account when we talk about food and the eating of it. So gluttony does not refer to a simple desire for food or for eating or drinking: It refers to an inordinate desire for food and drink.

THE COMPANY GLUTTONY KEEPS

The sin condemned in Scripture as gluttony is identified by its companions. The warning against gluttony in 1 Cor. 6:9–20 is couched in the middle of a passage concerned primarily with fornication. As we turn to the Old Testament, we see the same thing. We must understand that these kinds of sins go together.

Exasperated parents

In the book of Deuteronomy, we see what happens when parents of a glutton bring him in. "And they shall say unto the elders of his city, This our son is stubborn and rebellious, he will not obey our voice; he is a glutton, and a drunkard" (Dt. 21:20). Notice in verse 20 that this son is identified as a glutton, but also notice that he is defined as a drunkard and rebellious as well. When his parents try to deal with him, he rebels and won't allow them to have anything to do with him.

The word translated here as "glutton" (*zalal*) refers to riotous eating, orgiastic eating; the kind of eating you would see and not be surprised to find associated with sexual immorality and other kinds of disorder. This is the context, and this is why the penalty for this sin is so strong. This sin warrants the death penalty—it was not a case of having an extra candy bar.

The end result

A glutton will come to poverty. "Hear thou, my son, and be wise, and guide thine heart in the way. Be not among winebibbers; among riotous eaters [gluttons] of flesh: for the drunkard and the glutton shall come to poverty: and drowsiness shall clothe a man with rags" (Prov. 23:19–21). The end result of gluttony is poverty. This was the sin of the prodigal son (Luke 15:13). He ran off to another country and wasted his father's substance in riotous living. So gluttony is not reaching for that extra cookie. This is not to say that such cookies have nothing to do with your sanctification, but it is not what the Bible is talking about when it refers to gluttony. Gluttony is overtly shameful behavior.

Shameful behavior

"Whoso keepeth the law is a wise son: but he that is a companion of riotous men shameth his father" (Prov. 28:7). It is interesting how often the texts talk about sons and men. It is bad enough to be a glutton on your own, but it is just as bad to be associated with people like this. Even to be associated with gluttons brings shame on the fathers of such sons.

FATNESS AND GOOD CHEER

Our culture defines things differently than the Bible does. The Bible uses the image of fat very differently than do we. In fact, in Scripture, leaving aside the fat of the sacrificial offerings, there are two basic connotations of fatness. One is that of insolence and rebellion (Ps. 17:10; 73:7; 119:70; Is. 6:10; Jer. 5:28; Job 15:27). And the other—somewhat surprising to natives of this fat-free culture—is that of abundant blessing (Gen. 27:28; 45:18; 49:20; Num. 13:20; Dt. 31:20; 1 Chron. 4:40; Ps. 22:29; 36:8; 65:11; 92:12–14; Pr. 11:25; 13:4; 28:25; Is. 10:16; 25:6; 55:2; 58:11). When God brought the people into the Promised Land he promised them a land flowing with milk and honey. It is a picture of abundant fatness. We need to recover a biblical way of thinking so that the images the Bible represents to us are not seen as gross, but rather lovely.

Wonderful blessing

So when we think of fat, we should think of God's wonderful grace. "And they took strong cities, and a fat land, and possessed houses full of all goods, wells digged, vineyards, and oliveyards, and fruit trees in abundance: so they did eat, and were filled, and became fat, and delighted themselves in thy great goodness" (Neh. 9:25; cf. 8:10; 9:35). Clearly our standard cannot be the modern loathing of fat in every form.

On the one hand, the arrogant are clothed in fat (think of Eglon in Judges 3:17). They have given themselves to gluttony and rebellious eating and have made themselves fat. But fatness is also a blessing when it is given from the hand of God. So, you have proud fat and humble fat. You have grasping fat and you have receiving fat. You have fat that soars higher, and fat in the fire.

"Gluttony" in reverse

We have already noted the fat-phobia of our culture. There is a spiritual danger here. The Bible attacks those whose god is their belly. A glutton is a belly-god. "For they that are such serve not our Lord Jesus Christ, but their own belly" (Rom. 16:18). They are not serving God, they are serving their belly. You have a similar comment in Philippians 3:18–19. So, gluttony is the pursuit of these sensations *apart* from acknowledging God and receiving his blessing. And when you seek to get these sorts of feelings from things like food, you are not going to be constrained in other areas of morality. This is why gluttony is joined together with other forms of licentiousness; drunkenness, fornication, adultery, etc. This is also why when pagans try to get away from these kinds of sins they adopt ascetic practices generally. So, pagans love to get drunk but when they see the result of alcohol abuse, they love to ban alcohol. Similarly, when they see the effects of gluttony, they try to ban foods. Both are forms of paganism. This is why, in paganism, you have groups of people devoted to getting drunk and then in reaction to that you have other groups devoted to tea-totalism. Or you have sexual licentiousness giving way to total abstinence. When you have people giving themselves over to their various lusts you also have lusts in reverse.

Ambrose Bierce in *The Devil's Dictionary* defined rum as a substance that causes madness in total abstainers. This madness goes both ways: if you drink it, it makes you mad, and if you don't drink it, it makes you mad. People can't comprehend that God might give a wonderful gift. But these kinds of lusts are never successfully checked by any kind of asceticism. Asceticism does nothing valuable in fighting the god of your belly. Refusing to give your belly anything is still focused on your belly. You're still serving your belly, but in the other direction. These are the commandments and doctrines of men, but are of no value in restraining the flesh (Col. 2:23). Americans have a deep faith in salvation through food. Either that, or no food. But Jesus taught that foodstuffs cannot defile a man (Matt. 15:17). You cannot become more godly by what you eat. You godliness might determine what you eat, but you cannot become more godly by eating anything. If your attention is drawn to your belly all the time, whether you eat or not, your god is your belly.

SELF-CONTROL

Godly self-discipline is a result of the Spirit's work in our lives. And so we return to 1 Cor. 6:9–20.

All things are lawful

Look to the motive, not the food (v. 12). There are certain things that the Bible tells us we can learn from nature. We know that jumping off cliffs teach us a lot about sudden impact death. In Verse 12 we are given a principle that we can apply to other things. For example cigarettes are not prohibited in the Bible. It is lawful for us…up to the point where we become enslaved to it. What makes it lawful or not is not whether you take it in, but what your motive is. Are you serving God? Or are you serving your own stomach? Paul says that he will not be brought under the power of any, and so it is hard to imagine him lighting up.

God will destroy both the belly and food in their current form (v. 13). So, enjoy your food in the light of eternity.

Practical considerations

Of course, if you want to lose weight for practical reasons—being able to tie your own shoes, that sort thing—then it should be encouraged. Then, you should do what you want. These are practical considerations. They don't address the theological or root questions. If your motives are right these kinds of things should be encouraged. But you should realize that we live in a culture that idolizes food and weird teachings about food.

And people like to kid themselves and deny that what they are doing is what they are actually doing. There was a sociological study where a group of people were asked to write down everything they ate for three weeks. No one lost any weight. For the next three weeks the people conducting the study fed the same people what they had recorded that they had eaten and in that three week period . . . and they lost weight like crazy. If they said they ate a Snickers bar at 2:00 pm, they were fed a Snickers bar at 2:00 pm. The problem is that people lie to themselves.

THE ANTIDOTE TO ALL SIN

The sin of gluttony is therefore two-fold. One is a lack of self-control with food—compulsive, driven behavior with food. The other is a finicky compulsion over food. The solution to both problems is not a new resolve to set up a new menu for yourself. The solution is to learn how to sit down at Christ's table (1 Cor 10:15ff). He has provided the fare—the bread and the wine.

We cannot eat at the same table where the demons eat. There is not a third table. There is no third way. There is nothing in between. Everything edifies if done with the right motives. So, draw near to Christ, sit down at the Lord's table and eat anything you want to eat… as long as you are eating in faith. The table of demons wants to bind your conscience and keep you from enjoying the blessings of God as you sit down to eat.

The way you sit down at the Lord's table shapes the way you live your life outside of the table of the Lord. You are to sit down at the Lord's table and think rightly about the Lord's food and it will come to change the way you think about everything else you eat. How you are oriented to the Lord's Table will shape how, or whether, you sit down at another table.

In Christ, everything you might eat is clean—you don't need a list. If you are eating in the Lord, anything you eat is good for food. But if you aren't in fellowship with Christ and eating in faith, everything you touch will be spiritually contaminated. The answer is that if you are eating in faith, you can give thanks for anything and therefore you can eat anything and drink anything. Whatever you do, in faith, you should do to the glory of God. If you can't eat it to the glory of God, don't eat it. Looking at the package won't solve the problem. Looking at Christ in faith solves the problem. Do all to the glory of God, for all things done in faith are lawful.

ENVY

A sound heart is the life of the flesh: but envy the rottenness of the bones. (Prov. 14:30)

INTRODUCTION

Envy is a difficult sin for us to address in the modern era because in many cases we have made it into a virtue. There are many sins we still recognize as sins, but many times our people embrace envy in the name of justice or rights or equality. Envy is a creed or way of life form many in America today. We have inverted the moral order. Jesus told a parable about the workers hired at different times to work in his vineyard. The owner of the vineyard went out at different times of day to hire more and more workers, all hired to work at the same rate. When the day was over the workers who had worked the whole day thought they ought to make more money than those who had been hired only a couple of hours before the work day was over (Matt. 20:1–16). We would tend to see this as the basis of a class-action lawsuit because we look at it sideways. We think it isn't fair that others would work for a shorter amount of time and get paid the same as we get. It isn't fair, or right, or just. But Jesus told this story to make a spiritual point: God can do what he wants with His money. He paid the people exactly what he said he would pay them and which they agreed to receive. But our culture views this event in the light of envy. "That other guy is getting something we aren't." "He didn't work nearly as long as we did and he's getting the same amount of money as we got. That isn't fair." This is how laws are expounded by people who are envious.

A sound heart is the life of the flesh: but envy the rottenness of the bones. Envy debilitates. Envy takes you down. Envy saps your strength. Envy makes it impossible for you to function effectively in the world. Envy is a rottenness in the bones.

Our culture thinks that the solution to the sickness of our society is the medicine we take, but that medicine is actually the cause of the sickness. Envy cries, "that's not fair." Envy cries, "I have rights." Envy cries, "I have to get what's coming to me." "I'm just standing up for what is rightfully mine." This "medicine" is the disease, the sickness, the poison. It isn't what is going to make you better. Envy is rottenness to the bones.

THE PRINCE OF SINS

Pride, which we have already considered, is the king of sins. But if this is the case, then envy is a prince. What is envy? The word refers to a malicious regard to the advantages seen to be enjoyed by others. Covetousness is happy to let another person have a thing, as long as I get one for myself. It is simple avarice or greed. While covetousness would be content to duplicate the blessing that another person has, envy has a destructive side. I don't simply want to acquire what you have—if I don't have it, I'm willing to take you down so that I can have it. And if I can't have it, even then, I'll still take you down—so that at least you can't have it either. This is the malicious, biting, devouring side of envy.

And if we deck it out as a virtue, we're not going to tell ourselves we're now being envious. If we were to say that I'm treating my sister this way because I'm being envious, the gig would be up. We know that envy is listed as a sin in the Bible and that isn't a good thing. So we camouflage it, hide it so that we can pass it off as something else. We even camouflage it as a zeal for righteousness or dress it out as a prayer request. But the edge to take down, to put those other guys in their place, to see them humbled instead of built up, no matter what we call it, is not righteousness at all. It is envy and it is grievous sin.

Envy attempted fratricide

What motivated the fathers of Israel to treat Joseph in the way they did? Stephen answers the question clearly for us. "And the patriarchs, moved with envy, sold Joseph into Egypt: but God was with him" (Acts 7:9). The patriarchs, moved with envy, were so malicious in their spite toward Joseph that they were willing to bring their father's "gray head down to the grave in sorrow." They were willing for him to think his son had been destroyed. Many of the brothers were willing to kill Joseph but because not all were willing to go that far, they ended up selling him into slavery in Egypt.

Envy can corrupt to this point. Brothers can turn on one another. Families can be ripped apart, up to and including murdering each other. These were the founding fathers of the nation of Israel and yet they were totally consumed with envy.

Envy persecuted the Apostles

"But when the Jews saw the multitudes, they were filled with envy, and spake against those things which were spoken by Paul, contradicting and blaspheming" (Acts 13:45). When the leaders saw the multitudes they saw it as a competition. Paul was winning the competition because he was getting more people to follow him. When they saw the multitudes they were filled with envy and they began to oppose: "contradicting and blaspheming."

"But the Jews which believed not, moved with envy, took unto them certain lewd fellows of the baser sort, and gathered a company, and set all the city on an uproar, and assaulted the house of Jason, and sought to bring them out to the people" (Acts 17:5). Envy persecuted the apostles. The religious leaders were envious that the gospel which the apostles preached was powerful and potent and it was changing the lives of men. It was changing the world. Envy will always resist the powerful working of the gospel, and envy will want to steer that gospel itself.

Envy murdered Jesus

The worst crime in the history of our race was perpetrated because of envy. Envy murdered Jesus Christ. "For he [Pilate] knew that for envy they had delivered him" (Matt. 27:18). Jesus was delivered to the Roman rulers because of envy. He preached in a way that the leaders could not preach. He led men in a way that they could not lead men. He healed others in a way that they could not heal. He could do all these things that they could not do. They could not outdo him in argument. He was not seminary-trained. He wasn't trained in any of the schools of the rabbis, yet He could run circles around them when it came to the application of the Scriptures. He could stump them at every turn. He could do everything better than they could. But instead of recognizing who He was and falling at his feet, instead of glorifying God because He had raised Jesus up, they turned on him in envy and they murdered him.

Not surprising

The Scriptures teach us directly that envy is a formidable sin: "A stone is heavy, and the sand weighty; but the fool's wrath is heavier than them both. Wrath is cruel, and anger is outrageous; but who is able to stand before envy?" (Prov. 27:3–4). Here are the stair steps: A stone is heavy and sand is even heavier, but a fool's wrath is heavier than both of them. But compared to envy, nothing even compares. When envy gets to work there is no reasoning or dealing with it. Envy is intent upon destruction and driven by malice.

NATURE AND DIRECTION

Interestingly, the envious pay attention to more than just the godly. A person who is envious does not just envy the righteous—they envy everyone, even other envious people.

Envy in two directions

"Devise not evil against thy neighbor, seeing he dwelleth securely by thee. Strive not with a man without cause, if he have done thee no harm. Envy thou not the oppressor, and choose none of his ways. For the froward is abomination to the Lord: but his secret is with the righteous" (Prov. 3:29–32). If the oppressor is pillaging and taking things and he seems to be getting the good things in life and to be somewhat of a big man, don't envy him. You ask, "Why does he get away with that? Why does he seem not only to get away with that, but he is also blessed by God when he does it?" But the temptation to live your life this way is not good: Don't do evil against your neighbor, and don't envy the oppressor.

The Bible says: "Let not thine heart envy sinners: but be thou in the fear of the Lord all the day long. For surely there is an end; and thine expectation shall not be cut off" (Prov. 23:17–18). Envy can operate in two directions. You can see a righteous man doing a great work for God and you can see that God is blessing his work, and you can be tempted to envy him. Or you can watch a sinner doing the things sinners do in their arrogance and rebellion. You can see what appears to be God's hand of blessing on his life and that he appears to be profiting from his evil lifestyle and you can be tempted to envy his life also. Whether or not you have something God has given to another—good looks, great brains, money, fame, etc.—you do not have the right or freedom to envy that person. You cannot demand that God give you what He has not given you. And you must thank God that he has apportioned to men what He has apportioned to them and be grateful for what He has given to you.

So, don't envy godly men or evildoers. It makes no sense to envy the rebellious anyway. You wouldn't envy someone who was getting on a plane that was going to crash in spite of the fact that they get to fly somewhere. The plane is going to crash. Neither should you envy someone that you know is going to get what God has in store for those who live their lives in rebellion against him. Don't envy the sinner.

Comes to nothing

Many men have envied, for many centuries. And where are they and their malicious wants now? "For the living know that they shall die: but the dead know not any thing, neither have they any more a reward; for the memory of them is forgotten. Also their love, and their hatred, and their envy, is now perished; neither have they any more a portion for ever in any thing that is done under the sun" (Ecc. 9:5–6). Their envy is gone. Envy is temporary and transitory. Envy cannot last. Everything under the sun, particularly our lusts, our covetousness, our envyings will be burnt up. All these things are temporary. We are told in the Scriptures that we are to live for that which is eternal. What is eternal? "The grass withers the flower fades, but the word of the Lord endures forever." So we are to invest our time and energy and our thoughts as we focus on the word of God. And we enjoy all the things around us that God has given to us in the light of God's word. The word of God sanctifies all things, Paul says. The Word of God governs and directs our lives.

JUST PLAIN WRONG

The Scriptures list envy together with a host of other evils. And just going to church does not make the evil disappear. In his letter to the Philippians Paul tells us that "Some indeed preach Christ even of envy and strife; and some also of good will: The one preach Christ of contention, not sincerely, supposing to add affliction to my bonds…."(Phil. 1:15). Notice that these were preaching Christ, some with good motives so that Christ would be proclaimed and others were preaching out of envy and strife so that Paul would get into more trouble while he was in his bonds. But since Christ was preached, Paul rejoiced.

Envy has come into the church in the same way that every other sin comes into the church—through the human heart. We have to deal with our own remaining corruptions, despite the fact that we are a converted people; despite the fact that we have new hearts; despite the fact that God is at work, building us up and conforming us to the image of his Son, Jesus Christ. There are remaining corruptions in all of us. And part of that corruption tempts us to look sideways at others who have got it better than we have it. Envy tempts us to want to see that others have more than we have and we want to slap it out of their hands and maybe take it for ourselves.

Outside of Christ

What is it like to live outside the covenant of grace? "For we ourselves also were sometimes foolish, disobedient, deceived, serving divers lusts and pleasures, living in malice and envy, hateful, and hating one another" (Tit. 3:3). And of course, we see the same thing elsewhere (Rom. 1:28–29). These people were living in malice and envy, biting and devouring one another. This is also why America is such a litigious society. We want what the other guy has and so we devour one another. We grasp at what he has but we don't. We live like this and we think this is honorable and right and true. But it is not. It is sin.

Divergent Teaching

And within the Church, we sometimes find competing doctrines (1 Tim. 6:3). The Bible tells us to divide ourselves from those who would fight against the words of Christ. If someone comes along and teaches other things than the gospel proclaims and lives an envious life, we should depart from him. We should strive to cling to the gospel, to hold to the gospel, to preach the gospel, and to embrace the gospel. We sit down around the table of gospel and enact by God's grace the gospel in the Lord's Supper. And when people see this begin to take hold and begin to have influence, they will set themselves against it and they will begin to rail.

THE ANTIDOTE OF ALL SIN:

In this fallen creation, we have a tendency to envy. But God, James says, gives more grace (Jas. 4:5–6). We need to know, before we look at that antidote, to realize that the first place a temptation to envy will come from is our own heart. James says that our spirit lusteth to envy. This means that every one of us will tend to envy when the opportunity arises. But God will give more grace than we have envy. In verse 6 it says that he gives grace to those who envy. Where and how is this grace given? He gives this grace to the humble. But we should not look primarily at what we must turn away from. Repentance is not just turning away from sin, but it is also a turning to the correct thing. Rather, we turn to Christ, the one who restores and edifies us. The opposite of envy (zeal to destroy and wreck) is a zeal to build, to edify. We do this by clinging to Christ our Head (Eph. 4:15–16).

Envy bites and devours. It destroys and tears down. But true love builds up. It edifies. God has given gifts to the church so that the congregation might be built up as we allow him to work within us. We must cling to Christ in love.

PRIDE

Love not the world, neither the things that are in the world. If any man love the world, the love of the Father is not in him. For all this is in the world, the lust of the flesh, and the lust of the eyes, and the pride of life, is not of the Father, but is of the world. And the world passeth away, and the lust thereof: but he that doeth the will of God abideth for ever (1 John 2:15–17).

INTRODUCTION

In the garden, the woman saw that the tree was good for food, pleasant to the eyes, and able to make one wise (Gen. 3:6). This is how we may summarize worldliness—belly, eyes, and fevered brains.

Every sin that can be committed is traceable back to pride. Every sin has its foundation, its point of origin, in pride. Boil all the sinful meat off, and what you have left are the bones of pride. In out text, John defines worldliness for us. Here he is referring to the world's system, the way the people who are estranged from God behave in the world—what we call worldliness. He divides worldliness into three categories: the lust of the flesh, lust of the eyes, and the pride of life. It is interesting that John gives this list at the end of the Jewish aeon. But we can also see it in the beginning when Eve sinned in the garden (Gen. 3:6). She saw that there were three things about the fruit that were appealing to her: it was good for food (lust of the flesh), pleasant to the eyes (lust of the eyes), and would bring wisdom (pride of life).

So we see that this is a good biblical summary of worldliness. It is pride at the essence. God defines what is good and evil, and man thinks he knows better. God says, "Don't eat from that tree." And the man says, "What do you know? I know better than you. Let's talk about this for a minute." In every way and at every time man is competing with God and trying to substitute God's wisdom with our wisdom. We try to choose man's word over God's Word, denying what God has in fact said. And this is pride.

THE HATRED OF GOD

This is a sin that God hates above all others. Six things God hates, seven are loathsome to Him. What is first on the list? "These six things doth the Lord hate: yea, seven are an abomination unto him: a proud look, a lying tongue, and hands that shed innocent blood . . ." (Prov. 6:16–17). Number one on the list is a proud look. Herod's murder of the innocents is third on the list. We can't fully separate the various sins on this list here because pride is at the heart of every sin. But overt pride, a haughty look, a nose in the air, obvious arrogance, is something that Lord condemns in a particularly contemptuous way. The Lord condemns it as proceeding, with other sins, from a filthy heart (Mk. 7:22). God insults the very appearance of the proud (Ps. 73:6–7). He does really hate it.

PRIDE AND THE POOR

How does God describe the prideful? "Behold, this was the iniquity of thy sister Sodom, pride, fullness of bread, and abundance of idleness was in her and in her daughters, neither did she strengthen the hand of the poor and the needy" (Ez. 16:49). God says that the proud are contemptuous of the poor. The arrogant refuses to reach out to the needy, to help the downtrodden. Most of us know that the presenting problem with Sodom was homosexuality, but it was also pride and fullness of bread and an abundance of idleness. Proud and self sufficient, they thought it beneath them to care of the poor and needy.

Consider the same thing from another angle: "The wicked in his pride doth persecute the poor: let them be taken in the devices that they have imagined. For the wicked boasteth of his heart's desire, and blesseth the covetous, whom the Lord abhorreth. The wicked, through the pride of his countenance, will not seek after God: God is not in all his thoughts" (Ps. 10:2–4). The proud man boasts in his acquired goods. But God hates the proud. He hates those who boast in their possessions and who exult in their accomplishments. The essence of pride is that God is excluded from the proud man's thoughts. The proud only think of themselves and have contempt for anyone who tries to get them to think in any other way.

In our culture, in order to oppress the poor and needy we must announce loudly that we are going to help the needy. Then, in the name of social reform, we move in and destroy them. We see this same spirit of pride in the actions of Judas when he complained that the needy could have used the money that would have come from selling the ointment that was poured on Jesus' feet. He said he cared about the needy, but what he really cared about what the lining of his own purse. According to the Bible, the proud have contempt for the lowly, and so God has contempt for them in their twisted form of spiritual lowliness.

What wisdom hates we should hate

If wisdom hates something we should hate it. "The fear of the Lord is to hate evil: pride, and arrogancy, and the evil way, and the froward mouth, do I hate" (Prov. 8:13). We sometimes think that we should not hate, but this is to reject the words of God. We must hate sins, and, if this is true, we must hate the mother of sins—pride, arrogance, insolence. Love is a sin and hatred a virtue depending on what the object of your affections actually is. If it is sin, you must hate it. If you love sin, you are headed for destruction. If you love the world, you are in sin. Hating evil is righteous. Loving God is righteous, but so is hating what God hates. And God hates sin. Wisdom says we should hate what God hates. God hates pride, arrogancy, and the evil way. Therefore wisdom says we should hate those same things too.

Of course when we set ourselves up to hate pride the first thing we need to do is to look at ourselves. It is a natural thing for us to look at and see the pride of others, but if we want to do a really thorough job of it, we must begin by hating pride in ourselves first. If you hate the sin of others first, you are not loving the things God loves and hating the things God hates. This is because you are usually seeing in others what you are refusing to deal with in yourself. You are allowing your own haughty spirit to tell you that you are fine in comparison to others who have the obvious sin of pride. But you must begin by considering yourself first. Galatians 6:1 tells us to restore a brother caught in a sin, considering yourself first so that you won't be tempted. When you want to hate pride and arrogance, hate it first in yourself.

If we have considered ourselves first and acknowledged that we are tempted to fall in these areas, we are then required to help others who have been subjected to the same sins. Once we've removed the plank from our own eye, we are free and required to help our brother remove the speck from his (Mt. 7:5)..

JUDGMENT FALLS

Not surprisingly, God does not leave pride alone. "And I will break the pride of your power; and I will make your heaven as iron, and your earth as brass" (Lev. 26:19). God promises that he will judge sin. We think that nothing ever changes and we can wait until things go away and then life will go on in the way we want it to go. But God says he will destroy those who think they are independent from him. God sets himself against every form of pride.

Pride and shame

"When pride cometh, then cometh shame: but with the lowly is wisdom" (Prov. 11:2). Shame follows pride because there is a God in heaven and he judges the proud.

Pride and destruction

The Bible is plain here as well. "A man's pride shall bring him low: but honour shall uphold the humble in spirit" (Prov. 29:23). God does not leave the proud alone. He will bring the haughty down. And of course, there is that famous passage—"Pride goeth before destruction, and an haughty spirit before a fall" (Prov. 16:18). If a man sets himself up in his pride, he is asking God to smite him. God's hatred for pride is not passive, it is active and he will not allow insolent pride to continue.

Pride in office

In addressing the question of elder qualifications, Pauls says, "not a novice, lest being lifted up with pride he fall into the condemnation of the devil" (1 Tim. 3:6). Paul told Timothy to not allow a novice in the place of church officer. Tyndale translated that word as "young scholar." Do not allow a young scholar to be an elder of a church. This is because when an elder is a young scholar he is more likely to be lifted up with pride and will then be tempted to become diabolical. He will become like the devil when he fell—he was full of pride also.

God deals with pride wherever it manifests itself. If it manifests itself in the church, he deals with it in the church. So we need to avoid pride in all areas of life.

Calvinism and pride

We must prayerfully consider the issue of doctrinal pride. This pride comes to us because *we have the truth!* "We have the truth and you don't. We are truly worshiping God and you aren't." When it comes to the doctrines of grace, this is particularly insane—what do we have that we did not receive as a gift (1 Cor. 4:7)? God gave us the gift of understanding. God gave us all that we have. Moreover, it was a gift we did not want. But

God gave it to us regardless. We resisted it, we fought it, we insult it, we taunted it—just like those we try to tell about it now. But God gave it to us as a gift anyway.

Our Arminian brothers are far ahead of us in this. They understand that you can be proud of something you did, but you can't be proud of something someone else did. Too many Calvinists don't understand this. They think they can be proud of something God gave them. They are just like the Pharisee in this. We pray, "Thank you for making me such a wonderful theologian." And we go away just like the Pharisee—unforgiven (Luke 18). A proud Calvinist is an idiot. He doesn't really understand the doctrines of grace. God has given it to us as a gift of grace and then we turn around and act like it was something we earned. John Newton said:

> I am afraid there are Calvinists who while they count it a proof of their humility that they are willing in words to abase the creature and to give all the glory of salvation to the Lord, yet know not what manner of spirit they are of. Whatever it be that makes us trust in ourselves that we are comparatively wise or good so as to treat those with contempt who do not subscribe to our doctrines or follow party are a proof and fruit of a self-righteous spirit. Self righteousness can feed upon doctrines as well as upon works and a man may have the heart of a Pharisee while his head is stored with orthodox notions of the unworthiness of the creature and the riches of free grace.

It makes no sense at all for a man who is given a gift to be proud about having received the gift. Being proud in this way contradicts everything we say we believe. Paul says in Colossians that as the elect of God, we believe in God's predestinating grace. We believe in

God's goodness to us in these respects. But he says the uniform of a true Calvinist is tender mercies: "Therefore as the elect of God put on tender mercies" (Col. 3:12). If you are not clothed in kindness to others, you don't understand what you're affirming any more than the person you are trying to convince. And at least he understands that he gets credit for what he thinks he understands. You can't even claim credit for it, but you still have your pride.

This must be stated with great emphasis before the next point can be made.

Submission and sanity

Understanding who God is and gladly submitting to Him should be our very definition of what it means to be sane (Dan. 4:24–37). It is a sad thing when the pagan king of a rebellious nation knows his theology better than many in the modern evangelical church. We constantly write, sell, and produce products that proclaim to the world that we can do whatever we want with no consequences. We are out in the field eating grass like an ox. Our reason has departed from us. Our sanity has departed from us. Our worship has become trivial, lite, inane. This is all because we don't recognize what Nebuchannezzar recognized, which is that God is in Heaven and we are on earth. Nebuchannezzar asked the rhetorical question: "Who can stay God's hand? Who can say to Him, what doest thou?" The answer is of course that no one can. Not one creature among men can stay his hand.

It is a received and common doctrine in evangelicalism today that any one of us can stay his hand and stop him. He is coming to save us and we can say, "No, not me. Not today. No thank you." God invites you. The angels are sitting up in heaven singing softly, Jesus is Calling. Jesus is standing by the portals of heaven wringing his hands like some poor weak sister saying, "If only someone would come…" And we're saying, "No, no, no, not that way." "I'm not going to let you do what you want to do." "You're attempting to save me, but I'm not going to let you."

This is the heart and soul of modern evangelicalism, and the Bible defines it as insanity. It is madness, pride, arrogance. This is why we've lost our wits. This is why sanity has departed from the church. We don't understand what Nebuchannezzar understood and we will not understand it until God grants reformation to his church. When God grants reformation, he will also restore sanity to his church.

THE ANTIDOTE OF ALL SIN

What is the antidote to pride? The Bible teaching is that the answer is boasting. "My soul shall make her boast in the Lord: the humble shall hear thereof, and be glad" (Ps. 34:2; cf. 2 Cor. 10:17). The way we deal with pride is to learn how to brag, to boast. When we learn to brag biblically, the humble hear it and are glad. The antidote to pride is to boast in the Lord. The answer to pride is to glory in the work of another. If you boast in your own work and in your own efforts, in your own godliness and holiness, you've destroyed it all. You have substituted your own work, wisdom, resources for God and his Word.

Boasting is inescapable. We will boast. We will praise and honor. It is built into our being. The only question will be make our boast in the Lord or will we boast in man and his accomplishments. Does our gospel honor God or does it honor man? When it seeks to flatter man it is no gospel at all. What does our gospel do? Does it cause us to honor God or does it cause us to boast in man? The modern evangelical gospel seeks to honor man. It is man-centered. It caters to man. It wants to minister to man's "felt needs."

A God-centered Gospel boasts in what God has done. And when God acts in the world, his wisdom throws down man's vanity, man's self-sufficiency. The antidote to pride is to learn with Nebuchadnezzar to boast in the actions of another. The antidote is to realize that God is in heaven: God rules men.

www.ingramcontent.com/pod-product-compliance
Lightning Source LLC
Chambersburg PA
CBHW060534030426
42337CB00021B/4253